Pursuing an Audience of One

A 14-Week Guide to Spiritual Virtue

ONEIDA MARTIN

Copyright © 2015 Oneida Martin

All rights reserved.

ISBN: 0692443207
ISBN-13: 978-0692443200

DEDICATION

This book is dedicated to women everywhere. I pray that you are healed and made whole by the power of Christ—restored and made new by His word. This is a handbook which I pray would be a guide in your life to bless and cause you to excel into your joy unspeakable in Christ.

CONTENTS

	Acknowledgments	i
	Author's Note	1
	Introduction	3
1	Self-Esteem	5
2	Strength	13
3	Trust	19
4	Obedience	25
5	Healing	31
6	Love	39
7	Peace	45
8	Worship	53
9	Anger	61
10	Wisdom	67
11	Patience	73
12	Confidence	81
13	Un-mute	89
14	Victory	95

ACKNOWLEDGMENTS

To my parents for their love, support and life changing words in my life—without them I wouldn't be here.

To my Lord and Savior for this opportunity to share the gospel of Jesus Christ.

I am thankful to my pastors – Pastor Andre Faison, Pastor Artura Faison (who is also my sister) and Pastor Aurelia Greene (better known as Aunt A) for their impartation of Christ into my life. To my late Pastor Jerome Greene for the wealth of knowledge in Christ that he imparted—thank you.

To my KIR (Keep It Real) sisters: I love you ladies to life. No amount of words can express my gratitude and love for you ladies. I'm grateful for your undying love and support and your continued out-stretched hands toward me.

To my prayer partner, Cheriese, for constantly reminding me that there are books inside of me. I love you.

To my Spanish sister who constantly told me to step my game up and to come out of the box and be all that I can be. Love you, Monsey.

To my brothers: Holy Flava and Warrick Harmon for your consistent prayers, love, support, and belief in me. Thank you for your ability to help bring my vision to life. Love you Pastor Prentiss Harmon—you have been here since the inception of this book. Your belief in me, encouragement, strategic prayers, and friendship has helped to now birth and bring this book to life. Thank you.

To my church family: BCCPF for your prayers and support. Love you guys!

To my son, my heart, my baby: I love you more than words can say. Thank you for never doubting, for always believing in me, and telling me to stop being afraid to put myself on the market, and to let God do the rest.

To my nieces, Crystal and Chantel, for your love for me. All of your words of hope and encouragement have pushed me further. Love you guys.

To Tisha: for your love and support. Love you.

To my brother and sister in love: for all your prayers and encouragement. Thank you. Artie: for your help promoting my book. Love you guys.

AUTHOR'S NOTE

In case there are women who will set out on this 14-week journey and do not yet have a personal relationship with the Lord, a sinner's prayer has been provided for you. Read the following aloud:

God, I recognize that I have not lived my life for You up until now. I have been living for myself and that is wrong. I need You in my life; I want You in my life. I acknowledge the completed work of Your Son Jesus Christ in giving His life for me on the cross at Calvary, and I long to receive the forgiveness you have made freely available to me through this sacrifice. Come into my life now, Lord. Take up residence in my heart and be my King, my Lord, and my Savior. From this day forward, I will no longer be controlled by sin, or the desire to please myself, but I will follow You all the days of my life. Those days are in Your hands. I ask this in Jesus' precious and Holy name. Amen.

There is no greater privilege than belonging to the Lord. If you say it and believe it in your heart, another beautiful chapter will begin in your life. May His power rest upon you and work through you to break every chain and set you free.

**All scriptures in this book are from the NKJV (New King James Version), which is a resourceful tool in this pursuit and should be used as a companion to this book.

INTRODUCTION

To every woman who has been broken, scared, hurt, challenged, and distraught, I pray that the healing and wholeness that has been given to me be transferred to you by the power of the Holy Spirit. I know that our Lord has provided a great and mighty anointing to destroy every yoke in your life. Allow God into your circumstances so that you can be changed forever.

Are you happy? Are you facing setbacks? Are you overwhelmed? Is your heart aching? Do you feel like you have failed? Are you broken? Are you tired of being tired? Are you fearful? Regardless of what you are experiencing this is only a test.

The Lord put it on my heart to draw up a 14-week curriculum for anyone seeking an audience of our King—where He dwells in our presence and we pursue a deeply connected, intimate relationship with Him.

If you answered *yes* to any of the questions above, I believe this is for you. I identified myself in more than one of the questions. I've had terrible failures—even now as a Christian—and yet Christ is still calling me for a deeper walk with Him. If you wish to change things in your life, Christ will give you clear instructions on what you should do.

There are some tools needed for the next 14 weeks: **FAITH, HONESTY, HUMILITY,** and a desire to **CHANGE;** without these tools it will be difficult to be set free and to create a better you.

Each of the fourteen chapters will take you through a week-long experience. You will find scripture, declarations, and reflections to help narrow your focus. Don't rush through the lessons. Plan to go through only one lesson each week. Allow your tears to flow and your anger to be released. Whatever you do, purpose to not be the same as when you started. I am praying for a new and exciting you as I also pray for myself. Together, we'll go before the Savior for His divine wisdom and change.

SELF-ESTEEM
Week One

Scriptural Reference: Psalm 139:14 – I praise you, for I am fearfully and wonderfully made; Marvelous are your works, and that my soul knows very well.

Focus: I have found through the years that we do not love ourselves as we should; many situations occur and purpose to break us and destroy our character—hurtful words, painful experiences, tragic loss, and yet we continue to stand tall. While looking at your physical body—flaws, weight, and age—don't be ashamed of what you see. God knows everything about you. Get over your insecurities and love YOU until you can look at yourself without flinching, fear, anger and fraudulence.

> **INSIGHT**
>
> Self-Esteem is the art of loving yourself, or simply, how you view yourself.

I'm 49. I love the Lord. I consider myself to be smart and beautiful. Perhaps you're thinking, "Oh my! She is vain." I'm far from it. This was not always how I felt about myself; my view was totally different years ago. I hated myself; it made me angry when people would say, "You're so beautiful." The thought of beauty sickened me because nothing in me agreed with that at all. I hated my weight and my looks even when I was younger and was considered to be what this generation calls a "bad chick". I was absolutely clueless about who I was.

I was married young and I was oblivious about what marriage meant or how to enter into it. I hadn't been exposed to a lot of successful marriages so nothing registered. I was in a lifeless, non-committed relationship that yielded a lot of hate and brokenness. I love marriage. Please don't misunderstand me. It's wonderful and I can't wait to do it the right way. However, the levels of disrespect and disconnect that I walked through almost killed me. For the most part, in that relationship I was literally the "walking dead." I was bound, broken, fearful, intimidated, angry, numb, and hurt. If you can name it, I endured it. I lost a child at birth, dealt with infidelity, was overweight, and I felt incredibly overwhelmed. There were a few good days; however, they did not outweigh the bad.

The words spoken against and to me made me absolutely miserable. The deep and powerful impact and the weight of the words that fell on me were unbearable. I thought that if I helped others they would love me and I would feel better. To no avail, that didn't work. If someone would just love away the pain, that would help me greatly. The lies the devil whispered and the frustration in my soul coupled with the idea that I didn't really know Christ was a heavy burden. My mind had an idea of who He was, but my heart was void of any real intimacy with Him. I could only rely on people and their comments, thoughts and perceptions.

Never allow the words of another to shape, form or create you. You will be slave to their opinions of you and not know who you actually are. The Lord says He is the God that heals us and loves us. It's different when you know who you are and whose you are. You walk differently, talk differently, and see differently. Believe that there is a rest for those who love and trust the Lord. I believe all women are beautiful; we are merely tainted and broken in our ability to love ourselves. Physical appearance isn't all that reflects a woman's beauty. Having self-worth, a belief in God and others, love, compassion, and a willingness to help your sister be set free are all factors that contribute to a woman's beauty.

We have allowed ourselves to give birth to that which others have spoken. Some of us don't even recognize ourselves because we have become bitter, angry, frustrated, confused, deceived, arrogant and prideful. The list is a mile long. Step back and begin to look long at who you are and are not. Don't waste time reaffirming what others have said. Command your life to fall in line with what God says. Encourage yourself, strip down and look at *you*. Even your flaws are a part of your beauty. It's not your looks that attract people to you. It's what's inside you that beacons others to come.

Self-esteem begins with the inner workings of your heart and proceeds out of your mouth. It will then pour out in the presence of others. Far too long we have rested on the hope that if we wish hard enough, talk positive, talk long enough, we will get superb results. No amount of wishing brings about change. Fairy tales are nice but not real. The change comes from confronting *you*, dealing with *you*, trusting God, believing against all odds that you are more.

The Lord formed us with the words of His mouth and His thoughts. John 1:3 says, "In the beginning was the word and the word was with God, and the word was God." All things were made through His word. You didn't ask to be here but you are. It's your job to determine the outcome of your life. You are formed by the words of your mouth so be aware of how you speak. Believe what you say! Instilled in you is God's purpose for living abundantly, fully, powerfully, joyfully, fulfilled and in peace. Thoughts and words transcend your circumstances. Don't remain in a broken place. Look up, get up, and don't stop. Apply the Word as a healing balm and never turn back. It's not too late to begin, believe you have received all that is for you.

Christ can't fail and neither shall you if you look to Him. Allow Him to speak to the inner chambers of your heart, soul, and spirit. You shall live. This is the beginning of our journey; let's strive to obtain "an audience of One". Our Lord is waiting for us. We have a daily appointment with the Lord who has called us out of darkness into His perfected light. Nothing shall harm you even if you get hurt; no weapon formed against you shall prosper. "I'll see you at the top or from the top," my pastor, Andre Faison, says. Now ladies you must choose what it shall be for you. Remember we are in the service of our King.

Declare & Decree: Lord, I am Your creation—Your servant created by Your mouth. You have given me all that I need to be the woman I will be in You. I declare everything You have said for my life to be true and will manifest and come to pass.

Questions to Ponder
Week One

1. How do I define love? How does that compare to the way that the Word defines love (1Corinthians 13:4-8)?

_____
_____
_____
_____
_____

2. Can I say I truly love myself? In what areas can I love myself more? Why has this been an area of struggle for me?

_____
_____
_____
_____
_____

3. Do I invest into my own life as I should (physically, spiritually, financially)? In what ways can I invest further into becoming a healthy, well-rounded woman of God?

_____
_____
_____
_____
_____

4. Who does God say I am? Am I confident in who I know God has called me to be? Do I really believe the things God has spoken over my life?

_____
_____

5. What hinders me from being my absolute best? Past hurts? Disappointments? Be specific.

6. What steps must I take to become a self-assured woman?

7. Do I fear becoming the woman God called me to be? Are there personal desires that I believe are unobtainable? If so, what are my thoughts and fears?

8. Am I ready to let go of the old me (fear, doubt, hurt, etc.)? How can I become a woman other women can gage their lives by?

___

9. Even my imperfections will shape who I will become. Am I ready to accept myself—flaws and all? How can I embrace them?

___

10. How would I describe myself? What image have I created of myself? Do I believe it? How can I improve it?

___

REFLECTION

Locate scriptures on Christ's love for you. Meditate on them as they help you to heal of insecurities and brokenness.

For Example:
But God shows his love for us in that while we were still sinners, Christ died for us. (Romans 5:8) This scripture shows that even while I wasn't even mindful of His presence, God loved me, forgave me, covered me, and even waited. He saw something in me, even in a time that I didn't acknowledge Him, He LOVED me.

_____
_____
_____
_____
_____
_____
_____
_____
_____
_____
_____
_____
_____
_____
_____
_____
_____
_____
_____
_____
_____
_____
_____
_____
_____
_____

STRENGTH
Week Two

Scriptural Reference: Ephesians 4:32 – And to be kind one to another, tenderhearted, forgiving one another even as God for Christ's sake hath forgiven you.

Focus: This week's focus is on forgiveness, or letting go of hurts caused by those who left you, spoke ill of you, denied you, and lied to you. You are required by Christ to let it go. It is not an easy feat to release someone from your box of anger. It is even more difficult to love them in spite of their attack on your life. Unforgiveness causes you to be in bondage. It steals your joy and breaks you down until you become a living, breathing vegetable.

I will forgive and pardon the one who has hurt me most. I won't judge nor will I be a victim forever. I have purposed to be healed and allow Christ to put to rest that thing which came to kill me. Forgiveness is one of the hardest, most challenging requests to be made by anyone. Usually, we are inflicted by someone close who launched the missile that almost killed us. Once we began to regain consciousness from whatever was done to us we feel like a character from the pages of a horror story. Our lives take a dive into a horrible pit. We desperately try to understand "why me?" and "how come?" "What did I do to deserve this?" we ask. Simply put, we can't wrap our minds around the pain that has paralyzed us.

> INSIGHT
>
> **Strength can be defined as moral power or courage. For the entire week purpose to discover your areas of strength.**

From the age of 8 until I was 13 I was molested by a family member. My sexuality was birthed from these series of events. I didn't choose this; it was put upon me. I was supposed to be a good girl—wait until I was married and in love. How could I handle a lustful, loveless relationship when I was too young to understand what was going on? I was soiled, broken, and blamed for an adult's action by another family member. I can't begin to tell you how this shaped my life.

When perversion raised its ugly head, my relationships were never what they were intended to be. It is crazy how one act, or many repeated acts, will come to steal your voice. Even when you're speaking, you're silent. Who can you tell? How do you find joy? Is it even possible? Of course it is.

I'm so glad that Jesus is my Savior; He made something beautiful of my ugly life. I had to learn to forgive and let Christ repair my life. When things are birthed from the wrong place, we have a perverse and warped sense of what things should be. We have to go back to the drawing board. Forgiveness is a must. Forgiveness doesn't free the person or people from their own guilt or actions, but it allows you release your own mind and heart from the prison in which you live.

Ask the Lord to show you what's real. Allow God's love to rest on and through that which was inflicted upon you. We often search for an answer that we won't find or is difficult to explain. Someone else's wrong upon you doesn't just get up and go away. Allow Christ to teach you how to love and forgive. Don't be afraid and don't stay in this barren, broken place any longer.

Jesus said, "By His stripes we are healed" (Isaiah 53:5). We are not only healed from sickness; Christ has come to make us whole—complete in Him and wanting nothing. Maybe you can't face your abuser. Perhaps they passed away or doing so would just be too painful. Write their name on a sheet of paper and, in a letter, tell them how they hurt you and then throw it away. Keep a journal and unleash your rage and anger in your writing. Let it go until every chain that held you bound is broken. It is also important to forgive yourself.

Don't allow yourself to be bound another day. Get free! Don't allow words from others or your own mind to dictate the direction of your life. You are fearfully and wonderfully made by the Lord (Psalm 139:14). If you want to be free, get up, pray, cry, scream—just don't remain where you are.

I'm praying with you. As you heal, get a prayer partner, talk to the Lord. He hears all and knows all. This is your hour of freedom and healing. No matter how old the wound, give it over to God. He can and will restore the years the enemy has stolen away.

Declare & Decree: I forgive my abuser; I let them go in my heart. Lord, You have given me strength to overcome and be healed from the torment I have lived with for so long.

Questions to Ponder
Week Two

1. Identify areas of brokenness in your life. What are they? What motivates me to be healed?

   _____
   _____
   _____
   _____
   _____
   _____

2. How challenging is forgiveness for me? Has anything hindered me from forgiving others?

   _____
   _____
   _____
   _____
   _____
   _____

3. Am I willing to face the sources of past hurts? What are my fears and reservations associated with doing so?

   _____
   _____
   _____
   _____
   _____
   _____

4. How would I define torment and bondage? In what areas of my life have I been tormented or in bondage? Am I up to the challenge of being set free?

   _____
   _____
   _____
   _____

5. God can redeem me from the abuse that created bondage. Will I let Him? What steps am I willing to take to let Him do just that?

_____
_____
_____
_____
_____
_____

6. What prevents me from letting go of the people who held me captive through word or deed? Here is a list of steps I can take to remove the thoughts of past abuses.

_____
_____
_____
_____
_____
_____

REFLECTION

Find scriptures on forgiveness let them absorb into your spirit until forgiving becomes the norm.

For Example: *For if you forgive men when they sin against you, your heavenly Father will also forgive you. But if you do not forgive men their sins, your Father will not forgive your sins.* (Matthew 6:14-15 NIV) As much as I've been hurt, I may have also hurt others and am in need of my Father's forgiveness. I must forgive those who've hurt me in order to receive forgiveness from God.

_____
_____
_____
_____
_____
_____
_____
_____
_____
_____
_____
_____
_____
_____
_____
_____
_____
_____
_____
_____
_____
_____
_____

TRUST
Week Three

Scriptural Reference: Isaiah 26:4 – Trust in the Lord forever, for in the Lord Jehovah is everlasting strength.

Focus: This week's focus is to learn to rely solely on the One who can heal, save, deliver, set free, change and make new. Let Christ lead, guide and direct you into all truth. Allow His love to cover your heart and emotions. Never wavier, hold on to His unchanging hand. He can never fail.

We must trust in the One who made us—our Lord and God, Jesus Christ. Trust is very intricate and delicate. It can be difficult to trust those who we love and encounter daily, especially when we've been hurt by them. Forget about trusting a stranger. We are all guilty of doing wrong and the hurt we cause others causes them to not trust us. I know we would love to think that we are perfect but—news flash—we aren't.

> INSIGHT
>
> Trust means to be confident or to have faith in someone or something. This week, reflect upon the level of trust you have in God.

How do I put my heart into the hands of someone who may have failed or hurt me? Can I trust someone that I don't believe has my best interest at heart? Will others continue to trust me if I constantly hurt them? We must all begin somewhere. No one is perfect. I try to give others the opportunity I would want for myself. You can only give what you have. If it's not in you, you can't produce it. It's like telling a cat to give birth to a baby chicken. It's impossible.

You have to learn to trust yourself first. Believe in you. The Bible says, "Love your neighbor as yourself." Some of us don't love ourselves or trust ourselves. We must enter into God's presence for our next breath, another day, and cease every opportunity to grab hold of Him. His truth is what will correct our wrongs, heal our imperfections, destroy all improper thoughts and transform our lives.

Often times we will go a part of the way in healing. Somewhere in the middle we quit because it becomes too difficult. It can be so painful that we back up and pretend that things are okay. God doesn't always get the proper time to fix our wrongs. You and I must allow the root of our mistrust to be unearthed and destroyed. Be honest and allow God to fix your flaws in the light of His word.

How can you say that you trust Jesus if He can't fix you, heal you, change you, and establish your steps? Often we would rather run, pretend, escape, push aside the truth and accept a watered down version of life. It is never too late to start. Christ is waiting on you.

You may be like me and have failed many times. However, you must believe that at some point it will all change. You will no longer be shaped by the opinions of men. I declare that you are coming out.

With boldness you will trust your Savior with your whole heart. Ask Him to teach you to trust others who have hurt you. Trust yourself and let God's love make you clean. Produce trust in your heart. Replace hurt and bitterness with love and kindness.

It's time to rise up and enter into your rest. Can God trust you with His word, His gifts, His blessings, His corrections, etc.? Trust is a two way street to be travelled by all.

Declare & Decree: God will guide me. Regardless of what I see, hear, or believe, I know that He can't fail and He will uphold me forever.

Questions to Ponder
Week Three

1. What are some indications that I trust the Lord? What are some indications that my trust in God is not as strong as it could be?

2. How could I allow Him to lead me in spite of my fears?

3. What hinders me from trusting God completely?

4. Was there a time when I felt like God failed me while trusting Him? What happened?

5. Not trusting God in some moments has caused me heartache. What were those moments? How were they fixed?

_____
_____
_____
_____
_____

6. When I lack understanding, I will keep my trust in God by…

_____
_____
_____
_____
_____

7. Psalm 46:10 says that I should keep still and know that He is God. What does it mean to be still? What are some things that I can do to maintain a "still" life that trusts God?

_____
_____
_____
_____
_____

REFLECTION

Find scriptures on trust and let them invade your heart this week.

For example: *Trust in the Lord with all your heart, and do not lean on your own understanding.* (Proverbs 3: 5) In spite of my inability to fully understand everything that is happening in and around me, I will consistently trust God as I seek the understanding I need to rest over in Him.

_____
_____
_____
_____
_____
_____
_____
_____
_____
_____
_____
_____
_____
_____
_____
_____
_____
_____
_____
_____
_____
_____
_____
_____
_____
_____
_____

OBEDIENCE
Week Four

Scriptural Reference: Joshua 24:24 – And the people said unto Joshua, the Lord our God will we serve and His voice will we obey.

Focus: We must surrender our lives to Christ in obedience. We are called to adhere to His voice and follow Him. Very often I have chosen my own way and failed. You have to purpose to do His will and totally stray from your own way. Yield your life to the one who gave His for you.

Obedience is better than sacrifice. I have learned this lesson the hard way on so many occasions. Why obey when I can do it my way? I know no one thinks that except me (smile). There are some things you will never be able to get back if you operate in disobedience. Disobedience is very costly. God wants you to decide for yourself and make your own decisions. However, he gives us clear lines and boundaries to stay within.

Insight

To be obedient is to submit to authority. This week, think about the areas of your life that you have completely submitted to God, and the areas that you haven't. If you're unsure, pray and allow Christ to reveal some things to you this week.

I have experienced emptiness and shame because I didn't obey my Lord. The unnecessary heartache is not worth the moments of fleeting pleasure. Yes, I can say like Frank Sinatra, "I did it my way" and got nothing. The Lord had to step in and rescue my heart and mind from the traps, snares and setups that I imposed on myself.

Satan is waiting for you to walk on the wild side. It tickles me because as Christians we know most things and yet we have obtained nothing—no power, no peace, and we aren't effective. Women are called to birth things into the spiritual and natural realm. Often we give birth in the spirit to things that are stillborn because we didn't want to follow the plan of God. It's a baby but it's lifeless.

Our lives will produce many dead things if we attempt to do it in our flesh. Be careful when you decide it is too hard, too much, or too big to do it God's way. Jesus has called for us to be anointed—to destroy yokes in others' lives—yet we constantly need resuscitation because we are disobedient. Not obeying God says, "I don't trust you. I can't believe you." Why call Him Lord if He can't have total control over your whole life?

I speak for myself because I get tired of waiting and I run off ahead of Him. I'm just talking about me. *Everybody* obeys, I'm sure. Thank God for His mercy. I can't take advantage of His grace and mercy. If I caused it to dry up, it would kill me. Only the best will come from His plan for my life. I must only trust Him.

I'm learning daily to obey; it is the only thing that yields life. We will fail, make mistakes, and get tired. It does not, however, need to be that way. God is calling for faithful servants. In our last lesson I asked if God could trust you with His things. He won't give you things that He knows you will mess up. You have to stand on the word that has not changed or failed in the many years that it has been around.

Christ is not limited to anything but your disbelief. Lay down whatever is causing you to stray. It's not worth the consequences. We love material things and people more than Jesus sometimes—as if they could keep us. Nothing will bring you joy like Jesus. Walk upright before Him. Let your heart adore Him and allow Christ to break the chains of disobedience. I love that He will never let me fail. I will receive all that He has for my life.

I pray that you receive all that He has for you. Stop disappointing Him through disobedient behavior. The Lord knows all things; nothing we do will catch the Lord by surprise. Keep seeking to do His will. Obeying Him will bring you joy, peace, strength, power, wisdom, and knowledge amongst other great things. Don't let anything or anyone cause you to become sidetracked. There are real rewards to be obtained in earth and in heaven for hearing, loving, serving and doing the work His way.

Declare and Decree: God, I will follow your Word for my life, and turn to it for direction. I declare I will live as you called me to. I decree I will learn to obey in all areas of my life.

Questions to Ponder
Week Four

1. What are some of the challenges I face when it comes to obeying God?

2. What are some things that have happened in the past as a result of doing things my own way?

3. What causes me to choose my way over God's?

4. Is obedience really better than sacrifice?

5. What voices, pain, plans, hurts, gifts, and desires have stopped me from obeying His voice?

6. What is the importance of obeying Him?

7. Is there anything worth disobeying God? What is it?

REFLECTION

Find scriptures on obedience and study them until obeying becomes the norm.

For example: *Why do you call me 'Lord, Lord,' and not do what I tell you?* (Luke 6:46) In order for Jesus to truly be Lord of my life, I must surrender all to Him and obey His commands. I must seek Him through prayer and fasting and yearn to only do His will. When I call Him "Lord," I want to mean it.

HEALING
Week Five

Scriptural Reference: Psalm 107:20 – He sent His word, and healed them, and delivered them from their destructions.

Focus: This weeks' focus is on healing. God said that by His stripes we are healed. For every lash Christ bore on his body while on the cross, healing was produced for you and me. We were delivered from sickness in the body, mind, and spirit. We are not bound to crutches, canes, mental torment, and diseased bodies. Healing was provided the day Christ gave His life for us. Suffering is not an option if we believe we have already received healing. We may experience some obstacles, but healing is available to all who have hope in their God and Savior.

I am healed on every level: mind, body, soul and spirit. This topic is close to my heart. The Lord allowed me to experience the power of His healing hands on several occasions. Many times my life could have ended—but God! Christ has touched every part of my person and delivered me. I remember the death of my second son.

> **INSIGHT**
>
> *Release* means to free from confinement, bondage, obligation, and pain, or simply, to let go. This week, purpose to discover what must be released from your life.

In my seventh month the doctor discovered that my son was missing the top part of his head. The only sign of life was an occasional slight flutter of movement. This was due to the connection of the umbilical cord. I had gained twenty pounds in two weeks' time. The doctor assumed I would have twins.

A sonogram revealed the doomed baby inside my womb. After an examination, the news that my son wouldn't live was delivered. The Lord had already began to prepare me through my mom who operates in the prophetic. In church the Sunday before she said, "something is going to happen." Her words were intended to make us better, not bitter. Who would have thought I was the one Christ would use to be a vessel for healing?

Once my son arrived and his cord was cut, he was gone. I began to hemorrhage; blood was everywhere. At midnight the doctors burst into my room. They said, "you must have an emergency blood transfusion immediately." There was a panic in the air. My family was concerned, including my ex-husband and I.

In two weeks' time almost all of my blood was back. I'm told that it actually takes about four months for your blood to build back up in your body. I discovered that nothing is too hard for God. He is the restorer of life, and can heal whatever ails you. There is no disease, no pain, or ache that is bigger than my Lord. His goodness cannot be measured.

He can and will cause all things to bow down before Him. Pain in your body, in your heart, or in your life will cause you to think that Christ has forsaken you. You feel left out and abandoned when you're battling with your health. Don't let your flesh tell you that the Lord isn't real or that He doesn't love you. Your body was healed on the cross.

Though the outward man perishes, he is healed. Some of us have sick hearts and minds, but they are healed also. Christ has defeated the devil on every level. It may not seem like it but it's done. We have victory even over death. You are defeated when you can't grasp the fact that Christ has healed you mind, body, and soul. The power of life and death are in the tongue. Be careful what you say in spite of what you may feel.

Let me be clear, Christ is never working on anything; it is already done, fixed, and changed. We sometimes forget those words ***"IT IS FINISHED".*** Christ is always seated at the right hand of God waiting on you. With Christ all things are possible. We fail, we blow it, we are hindered, and we often make mistakes, but Christ in us gives strength and power to overcome. Stop trying to figure it out and just believe.

I pray healing prevails in your body. If you are fighting anything, I pray healing overtake you now and bring swift change for the best in your body. Hold on tight. The best is here right now, so don't lose the moment. It is important to worship—even if you feel terrible—worship. Your praise will yield miracles in your body.

Declare & Decree: The Lord has not given me a spirit of fear. I am well in my mind, body, soul, and spirit. My healing is here, and I will see it manifest. I Am Healed, I Am Whole, I Am Healthy and I Am Blessed.

Questions to Ponder
Week Five

1. If I am healed why do I still *feel* sick in my body or mind? What may be hindering me from the full manifestation of what God says I already have?

   _____
   _____
   _____
   _____
   _____
   _____
   _____

2. How could I better handle attacks on my mind or body?

   _____
   _____
   _____
   _____
   _____
   _____

3. How may I declare healing even when I *feel* sick?

   _____
   _____
   _____
   _____
   _____
   _____

4. Is there something that I am doing that opens the door for sickness?

   _____
   _____
   _____
   _____

5. I want to be made whole? What are the steps I must take to get there?

6. I've prayed and believed, but nothing has happened. What hinders me from manifested healing?

REFLECTION

Find scriptures on healing and stand on that word until your healing is manifest.

For example: *Fear not, for I am with you; be not dismayed, for I am your God; I will strengthen you, I will help you, I will uphold you with my righteous right hand.* (Isaiah 41:10) Fear is in opposition of faith when I have doubt that God is with me and has healed me during times of suffering or struggle. Today I commit to always leaning on what the Word says in spite of my changing condition.

_____
_____
_____
_____
_____
_____
_____
_____
_____
_____
_____
_____
_____
_____
_____
_____
_____
_____
_____
_____
_____
_____

Pursuing an Audience of One

GIVE
Week Six

Scriptural Reference: John 3:16 – For God so loved the world that He gave His only begotten son, that whosoever believes on Him shall not perish but have everlasting life.

Focus: This week's focus is love—loving ourselves and loving others. Despite our pain and frustration, we must be constant and consistent in love. Christ's love resulted in the giving of His only son, which became life, health and strength for our lives. We are called to love in great measure, so let your heart be renewed in his hands. Love is patient, kind, it does not envy or boast, and it is not proud. It's not rude nor self-seeking. It is not easily angered and it keeps no record of wrong. Love does not rejoice in evil, but rejoices in the truth. It always protects, always trusts, always hopes, and always perseveres. Love never fails. We must gain a real perspective on love.

> INSIGHT
>
> **Give! Be sure that you are giving to the best of your ability, which is the greatest indication of love.**

You found me while I was hiding. You exposed my heart for its inner most desire. A place where I thought I would never be seen. You came in and lay hold of me. Now my world is filled with joy and pain, fear and excitement. Places where I think it's safe, You are standing there.

With my eyes I see You laughing, working and planning, but I didn't want You. In the past you brought heartache and pain, confusion and strain. Now You're calling me to live and not give up. Sometimes I rush to You feeling confident and overjoyed. Other times I run from You wanting to go back and hide—staying safe, avoiding your stares, comments and complements.

Sometimes You touch me and everything inside me melts. Other times I want to fight and leave You there alone. I've found there is no place to go and You're not already there. No feelings escape Your touch. There is nothing that can be hidden, for You expose all. Sometimes I am happy that love looked for me and found me once again.

The power of love is overwhelming. It will cause you to wake up early and go to sleep late. Your heart will flutter and butterflies will fill your belly. You may think, "Please! What manner of fairytale is this?" However, there is a love that can touch the very core of your person. It can break chains off of your life. Being in love is an awesome blessing if you ever get to experience it in this lifetime.

Some never get to know the height, width, length and depth of love. It is on the wish list of many. Christ has such a perfect and undying love for us. His love came at the cost of the cross. Some of us don't even realize how much He loves us. Just one touch will dry up your tears and calm your fears. It breaks through barriers. It will come through the doors of a crack house, a bar, a broken relationship, a sick body and fill you to overflowing.

We must rush into His presence which is filled with a love and joy that will take your breath away. Love encompasses everything. Perfect love cast out fear. Love never fails, never has to compete, and it doesn't seek its own way. It compromises, finding the answer to all questions. It covers and brings a calm that can't be obtained naturally.

Many suffer from a lack of self-love. We seek something in another or from another that we can't give ourselves. Live, laugh, and, more importantly, love. If there is no special someone, that's okay. Christ loves you past your faults, beyond your needs. Love is an action word. It's what we are called to do—not feel.

Love fights for the right to be present. Love conquers hate on every level. It restores and fixes things that are broken. Don't allow anything to stop the flow of love within you.

Declare & Decree: *I love myself and others unconditionally. I will move past my hurts and overcome all obstacles to love. It's important to give love in great measure. My loving others is not based on them loving me.*

Questions to Ponder
Week Six

1. What are some indications that I truly love myself? What are other signals that indicate that I could love myself more?

   _____
   _____
   _____
   _____
   _____
   _____

2. How do I know that I truly love others? How can I demonstrate my love for others at a greater level?

   _____
   _____
   _____
   _____
   _____
   _____

3. What are some things that I can do to love others even when I've been hurt by them?

   _____
   _____
   _____
   _____
   _____
   _____

4. Has something from my past (or present) hindered me from loving fully? What was it?

5. Why is love so important? What would life be like without all the traits encompassed in love?

6. What are the benefits of loving unconditionally?

7. Why is self-hatred so prevalent in women? What could be done to overcome it?

REFLECTION

Look up scriptures on love. Let the love of Christ in your heart destroy anything contrary to His Word.

For example: *Anyone who does not love does not know God, because God is love.* (1 John 4:8) If God is love, and I was made in the image and likeness of God, then I must also possess each of the traits contained within love—kindness, forgiveness, patience, etc. I cannot say that I know Him if I don't purpose to love others.

_____
_____
_____
_____
_____
_____
_____
_____
_____
_____
_____
_____
_____
_____
_____
_____
_____
_____
_____
_____
_____
_____

PEACE
Week Seven

Scriptural Reference: John 1:12 – But as many as received Him, to them He gave the right to become children of God, to those who believe in His name.

Focus: This week we will focus on what it is that we believe. Do you believe what the Lord has spoken for your life? Do you really take His word literally? Do you know how to stand on His word and believe it until it comes to pass? Don't rely another day on what you're thinking and believe that God is God and what he has said is the truth.

Believe in Christ and you shall never be disappointed. There are so many reasons to believe Christ. He died for us, loves us, heals us, blesses us and protects us. Sometimes we abandon the Lord because he doesn't do what *we* require. He doesn't move fast enough. We need *Him*, yet we place demands and time constraints on Him.

> INSIGHT
>
> **Do you see a reflection of peace in your life?**

At times we can be so disrespectful toward the Lord. If we would only understand who He is, we would act differently. In His presence is the fullness of joy, but we complain about everything that's wrong. It's a true indication that we are not always in His presence. We want so much, however we want to put very little effort into attaining it.

Imagine if Christ treated us the way we treat him—taking breaks, getting angry or serving, surrendering and worshipping only when the mood is right. In the time of trouble we yell, scream, flip out and command an audience with our King because we're desperate for quick answers. I know Christ is long suffering. Many of us should be dead. Lord, forgive us of our ignorance toward you. Believe the Lord past your understanding—past your knowledge and wisdom.

Christ can't fail; He changes not. Everything you will ever need can be found in Him. If he said a thing, know that it will come to pass. His word is established and it will stand forever. All that we try in our own strength and power is like building a house on sand. It will surely fall.

The price of God's only son should be enough for us to hold on to. Instead, we challenge God's word with disbelief and constantly need signs and wonders. Get off the elementary belief level and mature in Him. Milk is for babies and meat is a sign of maturity. Start by getting in His face. Allow all dead works and belief systems to be burned up in His presence

Declare & Decree: I believe beyond measure that He wants the best for me. He has a purpose and a plan for my life. I will believe even when I don't understand or see His plans taking shape.

Questions to Ponder
Week Seven

1. What are some factors that make it hard for me to believe God?

2. In what moments is my trust and belief in God strongest? Weakest? How can I minimize the weak moments and increase the strongest?

3. What can I do if I struggle to believe because I can't see anything in the natural?

4. What circumstances have hindered my belief or faith in God? Have I gone to God for clarity, understanding, and wisdom regarding those situations, or do I allow them to fester and put a damper on my faith?

___

5. What could unbelief cost me?

___

6. What could I gain if I only believe God and His word?

___

7. What are some (or what would be some) indications that I trust God wholeheartedly?

_____
_____
_____
_____
_____
_____

REFLECTION

Look up scriptures on peace, meditate on them, and allow the peace of God to saturate every crevice of your life.

For example: *Great peace have they who love your law, and nothing can make them stumble.* (Psalm 119:165) If the key to walking upright with the Father is simply having His peace, then it seems incredibly easy to continue on in this walk. What hinders me from total peace? Why does this walk seem to not be as easy as it appears in the Word? Why is it so hard for me to truly believe it? Disappointment in people and unexplained circumstances once got the best of me, but I declare that today I'll seek the peace and understanding needed to go further in the things of God.

_____

_____

_____

_____

_____

_____

_____

_____

_____

_____

_____

_____

_____

_____

_____

_____

_____

_____

_____

Pursuing an Audience of One

WORSHIP
Week Eight

Scriptural Reference: John 9:31 – Now we know that God does not hear sinners, but if anyone is a worshiper of God and does His will He hears him.

Focus: This week's reflection is on hindered worship. Worship is not just a song or praise dance or music. It's a lifestyle that is birthed from your experiences. Life's trials will form real worship within us. We can't forsake our intimacy with God, which is a result of our worship. We must come to Him each day in spite of our circumstances, regardless of our bank accounts, families, or jobs. Our daily cry should be Isaiah 64:8, "But now, O Lord you are our Father. We are the clay, and you are the Potter and all we are the work of your hand." Isaiah 61:3 says to *put on the garment of praise for the Spirit of heaviness.*

> INSIGHT
>
> **Worship extends beyond the confines of the church. Worship is in our hearts and is reflected in our lives.**

David was a man after God's own heart. His worship caused demons to flee; he danced before the Lord until his clothes fell off. He publicly declared and decreed his love for Christ through the medium of worship. Worship is devised of many things, yet intimacy with God is most important. Intimacy is a level for which very few are willing to sacrifice. Worship is not just a song, dance or praise. True worship is a lifestyle developed through our everyday relationship with Christ.

Some worship is developed and birthed through very painful life experiences. You may have lost someone; something may have been taken from your person (rape, violence, molestation). Often times we abandon the Lord in an attempt to find out who, what, when, where, why and how of the matter. I know that sounds strange but we do it. The Lord holds the answer to all of our questions.

If He can't answer it, then the answer is nonexistent. The enemy sets traps for us. The devil constantly bombards us with the notion that the

Lord has failed us. To our own destruction we buy into the lie and soon find that we are being swallowed up by the one who attempts to kill us daily. Worship should be continual; it should come in waves like rushing rivers or seas—flowing out of us. You may cry, dance, wave, run, sing, jump or crawl; there is not a set way to enter into the presence of worship.

Allow the Savior to release it through you however He chooses. You may be shut down right now; maybe you haven't been intimate with Christ in a while. Perhaps you feel disconnected, frustrated, angry, hurt, or discouraged. Remember it's just a feeling. Feelings come and go; the only thing that remains true is Christ. When all is said and done, He will breakthrough and set you free. Give the Lord a chance to have your heart again. He will walk in the desert places of your life and flood it with the water of His word.

He is our daily provision. Love Him completely with your heart. Allow nothing to stop your flow of worship. Surrender your whole heart to Christ only. Worship is simply your constant desire to be one with Christ. You may have other obligations in life, but none should ever take priority over Christ.

Your true desire should be to abide in His presence daily. Jesus must be a continual recipient of your adoration. Let nothing separate you from loving and worshiping Christ completely and totally. Let's make worship our point of focus for life.

Declare & Decree: Lord, I worship and adore you. I submit to Your authority and love and my life reflects worship in every area. Worship is my highest form of praise for You.

Question to Ponder
Week Eight

1. What is worship? What does it mean to worship God in spirit and in truth?

_____
_____
_____
_____
_____
_____

2. Is worship reflected in every area of my life? What parts of my life do not glorify God? What areas do I refuse to submit to Him?

_____
_____
_____
_____
_____
_____

3. What must I do to establish true, heart-felt worship and intimacy with God?

_____
_____
_____
_____
_____
_____

4. Do I really reverence the Lord? In what ways do I fall short of honoring Him with my life?

_____
_____
_____

5. A relationship is defined simply as being connected. In what ways am I connected with God? Where's the disconnect?

6. Can I describe my life as mundane or rehearsed, or am I "just going through the motions?" Why? How can I break the routine of life and worship for a deeper connection with the Father?

7. Do I purpose to be unhindered and unleashed in my lifestyle of worship? How can I better understand the freedom of worship?

8. How may I better rely on the Lord as my refuge? What are the challenges of releasing my burdens to Him?

10. Am I cold and indifferent in any area of my life? Why? How might developing a life of worship build a warm, caring character?

REFLECTION

Locate scriptures on worship. Study them. I pray that through this process you will worship Him deeper and more intense than before.

For example: *I say to the Lord, "You are my Lord; apart from you I have no good thing."* (Psalm 16:2) God gives so freely, and I've come to the realization that there is little that I could give back to Him. Repayment is impossible, but I commit to worshipping the Father with all that is within me. He is my *good* thing, and from Him flows all other good things in my life.

Pursuing an Audience of One

ANGER
Week Nine

Scriptural Reference: Ephesians 4: 31 & 32 - [31]Let all bitterness, wrath, anger, clamor, and evil speaking be put away from you, with all malice. [32]And be ye kind one to another, tenderhearted, forgiving one another, even as God in Christ has forgave you.

Focus: This week's reflection is about anger. Anger lies in the bosom of fools. Why do we permit harnessed anger to cause sickness, bitterness, and frustration? Sometimes we can't be productive because we lose it being angry. Anger is destructive and opens a door for the enemy to slip in and destroy you.

Face your anger. What caused you to be so mad in the first place? The Lord is willing to walk with you back to the exact spot. You may have experienced the death of a loved one, a broken heart, or betrayal. There is nothing so horrible that the Lord can't fix it. This week, purpose to lay your anger down and take up Christ in your heart. Beware of the unseen traps of the devil. His desire is to destroy you. Remember, women are birthers—the entrance way into the earth realm. The enemy would love nothing more than to stop you in your tracks.

> **INSIGHT**
>
> **While anger has very little to no influence on others, it can be the angered person's greatest detriment.**

Understanding the source of anger is helpful. There is usually a deeply-rooted hurt that is beneath anger. Recognizing that anger is a natural response to injustice, mean spiritedness, and wrong-doing is important. Resentment and anger toward others and ourselves can destroy our health and peace. The hurts we have experienced, if not checked, can cause major problems for us.

I know what it is like to live, eat and sleep anger. We must be careful not to allow any open doors in our heart to remain. We have a right to be angry, but the bible says to be angry and sin not. We must allow the Lord to fight our battles. Nothing you do can settle the score with someone who hurt you. You can flip out, curse them out, fight or be violent. However, the Word declares, "Vengeance is mine, says the Lord, and I will repay."

Stop and think about what has been controlling you all of this time. You said you laid it down—until something is said or done that sends you reeling all over again. We blur the lines when we don't let go of things. Is it easy? No. Can it be done? Yes. With Jesus you can forgive, heal and start on a new path. Forgive! Let go!

We lose whenever we try to fight our own battles. I know life seems unfair sometimes. Was it fair for Jesus to go to the cross on our behalf? He laid it all down for us. We allow many things to trip us up. I have been angry about some things. In the end I had to let it go. After the rage, the verbal assault, and the frustration, I was tired of being tired.

Nothing is worth losing your soul. The Lord sees all; He knows who hurt you and made you angry. It's hard to lay down some things, but it's so worth it. We block our own blessings when we attempt to do what God is so graciously willing to do for us. You are responsible for forgiving and letting it go. It's a process; no one said it was easy. Anything that manipulates your actions controls you, owns you and has power over you.

You have to think, is this worth my mind? Is this worth the empty effort? Can I continue to allow such fury to dominate my life? It's a door for hell to enter in. Anger rests in the bosom of fools.

Declare & Decree: I am no longer a fool and the devil can't have me anymore. I refuse to carry this anger around any longer. I release anyone or anything that has caused me this pain. Lord, I owe you my life and I desire to live free of anger and affliction. Restore my joy, Lord, as I surrender my all to you. Thank you that you have heard me and I'm free.

Questions to Ponder
Week Nine

1. What has been the source of my anger in the past?

2. What are some immediate triggers for my anger?

3. What has created feelings of regret? How could I better avoid doing or saying things I would later regret?

4. What revisions could I make to my life that would yield a person who isn't easily angered and who is quick to forgive?

5. In what part of my life have I lost control? What steps might I take to regain it?

6. Are there painful issues that I refuse to address because it is difficult to face them?

REFLECTION

Find scriptures on anger. Allow them to wash over you and destroy every entrance that has been given to the enemy of our soul.

For example: *For man's anger does not bring about the righteous life that God desires. (James 1:20) In order to live righteously, my life has to be void of anger. Whenever I become angry, I operate outside of the will of God and He is not pleased. Lord, grant me the ability to allow offense to roll off my shoulder.*

WISDOM
Week Ten

Scriptural Reference: Proverbs 4:4-6 – ⁴He also taught me, and said to me: Let your heart retain my words, keep my commands and live. ⁵ Get wisdom, get understanding! Do not forget, not turn away from the words of my mouth. ⁶Do not forsake her, and she will preserve you, love her, and she will keep you.

Focus: This week's reflection is upon wisdom. The Lord states that if we ask for wisdom, He would freely give it and not withhold it from us. At times we forget and operate in ignorance and without purpose. We rely on our truth and believe what we see and hear. Wisdom makes one sensible; it establishes right patterns in our lives. It restores our wrong thinking. *My people perish for a lack of knowledge.* We are destroyed by wrong thinking and poor decisions. Let us seek to know God's heart and plan for us through obtaining wisdom. If we seek wisdom, we will be preserved and gain understanding. Live and produce the fruit of life. Wisdom will restore our right vision and lead us into purpose.

> INSIGHT
>
> **Wisdom is by far the most powerful tool for those who desire to remain in the will of God.**

King Solomon was the wisest king that ever lived. This was due to his request of the Lord to give him wisdom to lead the people. We think being wise means knowing lots of things that others don't know or obtaining more book knowledge than others. We must allow Jesus to fill us with His wisdom for every step we take, how we live, how we walk, and how we talk. All of our movement should be led, guided and directed by wisdom.

Our life's choices aren't always guided by wisdom. We've made numerous mistakes and experienced the horror that resulted from operating outside of wisdom. Don't allow your flesh to dictate how you live. The Lord says if we ask for wisdom He will freely give it to us. Request wisdom and ask the Lord to pour it over you. The fear of the Lord is the beginning of wisdom. Wisdom causes us to avoid the snares of satan.

Disobedience throws wisdom out the door. We can't ever rest thinking we have it all together. Wisdom causes us to discern good from evil. Wisdom will reveal God's absolute truth. Wisdom will allow you to seek wise counsel. Wisdom will always allow us to walk in the right direction. Don't rest in what you know; seek wisdom daily.

You won't ever be lead astray. Trust me, I know. I've operated in my own way and blew it each time. Being without wisdom is like the body without blood. Everything we need Christ has already provided. It's ours for the taking. We have to rush to the Lord and allow Him to pour it out over our lives and into our hearts so that we can lead others by example.

Declare & Decree: I choose wisdom to renew my mind and bring about perfect strength. I purpose to be wise and not foolish. I'm no longer content with faulty flesh moves and decisions. I purpose through wisdom to soar with the eagles.

Questions to Ponder
Week Ten

1. What does it mean to operate in wisdom? Do I always operate in wisdom?

2. What is my purpose? How can wisdom help lead me into my destiny?

3. How often do I make unwise decisions? What causes me to operate outside of wisdom or without first seeking the peace of God?

4. What does it mean to know that the Lord has purchased my life at a very high price? How does that affect my decisions?

5. What would I be like if wisdom ruled all parts of my life? What are the characteristics of a wise woman?

_____
_____
_____
_____
_____

6. Wisdom and disobedience do not mix. What things within me must be purged so that I can be fully led by wisdom?

_____
_____
_____
_____
_____

7. In what areas of my life do I operate in pride instead of wisdom?

_____
_____
_____
_____
_____

8. How often have I traded wisdom for my own self-absorbed ideas?

_____
_____
_____

REFLECTION

Locate scriptures on wisdom. Learn them and walk in them that they may guide you into God's perfect will.

For example: *If any of you lacks wisdom, he should ask God who gives generously to all without finding fault, and it will be given to him.* (James 1:5) If asking God for wisdom into every situation allows me to walk upright and is pleasing to Him, then it seems quite simple. There are times when I just want things my way and my patience is short. Lord, help me to seek You above all.

_____
_____
_____
_____
_____
_____
_____
_____
_____
_____
_____
_____
_____
_____
_____
_____
_____
_____
_____
_____

PATIENCE
Week Eleven

Scriptural Reference: Psalm 37:7 – Rest in the Lord and patiently wait for Him, do not fret because of him who prospers in his way.

Focus: Oh the power that waiting on the Lord brings! Sounds crazy, I know, because the last thing most of us want to do is wait. We live in a get it, move it, fix it, do it right now type of world. We want results that happens as quickly as heating up food in a microwave. In 5 minutes my frozen meal is done. I want my broken life restored in 3-5 seconds. Lord, I don't care what you have to do, just do it fast.

Waiting develops patience and faith. We become turned off if Christ takes too long. Our heart's cry becomes, "Why have you left and forgotten me, Lord? I trusted you." Now we lose all hope because He didn't move when we wanted Him to move and yet the Lord takes us through the process necessary to fix us. We didn't acquire our problems overnight, so why would we be foolish to think they would vanish immediately? Wait on the Lord and be of good cheer. "The longer the wait the bigger the blessing," a friend told me. Don't be afraid to wait. The Lord knows how, when, and what you need at all times. And no devil, no person, nothing will be able to stop Him from giving you what He has for you in due season. So live, love, move and submit to the Lord. I promise your waiting won't be in vain. He will establish you in the right moment in time. Don't allow anyone or circumstances to talk you out of waiting. Take it from a professional waiter—it will all be worth it.

> **INSIGHT**
>
> **Your ability to wait could mean the difference between receiving God's best and simply receiving.**

Wait on the Lord, and again I say, wait on the Lord. We get nervous having to wait on anything—especially the Lord. If God loves me, why do I have to wait? He is all powerful and filled with knowledge, wisdom, and truth. Can't the Lord move and do things fast? Yes, He can. Will He? Not all the time. Waiting requires skill and patience. We must remain confident and hopeful in this phase.

The questions that require God's answer will always fall into 1 of 3 categories: yes, no, and wait. "No" is painful because our flesh can't tolerate rejection. "Yes" causes us to skip off into the sunset because we get what we want. "Wait" sours in our mouths the moment we realize we can't have what we want *now*. We get stuck, frustrated, angry, resentful, and may even be determined to walk away.

As much as we would love to believe that we can do and have what we want when we want it, it is just plain wrong. It's like hump day (Wednesday); it's not the beginning nor is it the end of the work week. It's right in the middle. Maybe you didn't start off right but you can finish well depending on how you walk it out.

We become impregnated with an answer from the Lord. Sometimes he doesn't say *when*, yet we assume that tomorrow is the day. Years may pass and you find yourself questioning His *yes*. He did, and now you're being taught what is needed to obtain your request. Time belongs to man, eternity is God's. You've fainted, cried, flipped out, became discouraged and enraged and He is simply seated at the right hand of the Father. He's not moved, rushing, blinking, confused, nor wondering what's going on.

He's teaching, establishing, breaking, changing, healing, restoring, protecting and we are blowing it. We will get it right at some point. Even if we don't speak out loud, our thoughts are raging. *Didn't you tell me it was going to happen, Lord? How come you're not doing anything? You've got nothing for me? Why are you silent? Can't you see what's happening? Where's my breakthrough? Fix it!*

In my mind's eye I can see Him smiling yet slightly saddened. *They still don't trust Me. My children, I yearn for the moment when you will know that what I say is done.* Be careful trying to force the hand of God through pity. It might backfire. He can't fail, so if He says wait—wait. It will be more than you can ever imagine.

I know I've been waiting for a few things for a long time. I stopped crying and wiped my tears. Instead, I lifted my head, hands, and heart. I plan to commit my days to waiting until my appointed time. Oh it's tough, I used to fall out and have tantrums. Angry, lips stuck out, life out of order, and mad for having to wait.

Now in confidence—not in fear, anger, or bitterness—just in faith, I'm getting ready. Everything is on the verge of breaking forth, and I'm excited. God is good and greatly to be praised. So I encourage you to wait with cheer and joy. Knowing that God is going to bless you greater than you can imagine.

Wait on the Lord and be of good courage and He shall strengthen your heart. Serve while you wait, love while you wait, and give. Life isn't over or on hold. Your answer will arrive soon. Will you be ready?

Declare & Decree: I will wait on the Lord; I promise not to fear, be angry or moved. I will allow my heart to trust in Him forever.

Questions to Ponder
Week Eleven

1. What does it mean to wait? What does waiting entail?

2. Why am I typically in such a rush?

3. How has moving out of fear or frustration hurt me in the past?

4. What mistakes have I made because I refused to wait?

5. What are the costs associated with stepping outside of God's timing? Is that a price I'm willing to pay?

6. Would I describe myself as impatient? Anxious?

7. What are some things that I can do while I wait for the manifestation of God's promises?

8. What can I gain by waiting?

REFLECTION

Find scriptures on waiting. Commit them to your life that you may learn patience in your God.

For example: *But as for me I will look to the Lord; I will wait for the God of my salvation; my God will hear me.* (Micah 7:7) It is without question that God hears and answers every prayer. My commitment is to seek Him, trust Him, and wait for His perfect will for me.

_____
_____
_____
_____
_____
_____
_____
_____
_____
_____
_____
_____
_____
_____
_____
_____
_____
_____
_____
_____
_____
_____
_____
_____
_____

Pursuing an Audience of One

TRAGEDY
Week Twelve

Scriptural Reference: Job 29:15-19 - ¹⁵I was eyes to the blind, and feet to the lame. ¹⁶I was a father to the poor, and I searched out the case that I did not know. ¹⁷I broke the fangs of the wicked and plucked the victim from his teeth.

Focus: Deal with the tragedy. I wasn't supposed to talk about the rape, the molestation, the divorce, the accident, or the abortion. There are some very hard issues that we will face in this lifetime. There are things that may have caused our faith to flee, ripped out our hearts, or almost killed us, yet even if we are weak, angry, feeble, distraught, or confused, God is ready to walk us back to the place of death and resurrect us.

I know you don't want to think about it. Some of us never stopped thinking about it. It consumed our thoughts, numbed our emotions, and became a life-sucking vessel. *I can't breathe. I refuse to feel. I just exist. I tried but failed terribly. I wanted to fix it but it hurts. No one knows or understands.* I know I have lived through some horrific challenges from childhood molestation to a horrible marriage. The loss of my second son who was born stillborn without the top part of his head was traumatic. The challenges rolled in like a tide. I had to learn how to live one breath at a time.

> **INSIGHT**
>
> **At the root of every powerful testimony is a person's greatest test, greatest trial, greatest pain, greatest frustration, greatest loss, greatest agony.**

Who could know my plight? No one except the Lord who made me. Did He bring these circumstances into my life? No. However, He allowed them to touch me for the sake of helping others. I can hear someone say, "Not God. He wouldn't allow such horrific things to come upon someone." Read the story of Job and look at all of the Bible heroes. No pain, no gain. You will never learn how to fight, believe, trust, stand or obtain anything without life's lessons. I don't know who I'm speaking to, but God knows and He sees.

He's been waiting for you to allow His presence to come in and overtake you. I know it hurts, but you'll feel so much better when He is done. He will restore your joy. However, you have to want it. Don't be like the man at the pool of Bethsaida whom the Lord questioned, "Whilst thou be made whole?" He laid there for 38 years and didn't move an inch. He gave excuses for why he laid there. Very often we die, not physically, but mentally and spiritually at the place of tragedy. Lame women: stop making excuses and get up and walk; your healing has come today.

This week's lesson may be the most trying—dealing with the tragedy. Often times we avoid the topics that remind us of moments of incredible pain. Even our posture changes in the middle of the conversation. *I don't want to confront this*, we think. Jesus wants to take you to the place where you buried it, where you died emotionally, where that numb feeling took root.

This reminds me of a broken cup that has been glued back together. It is not quite right anymore. It's chipped, cracked, uneven, and after a while it can't hold the water. Whatever you put into it leaks out one drip at a time. When you put it back together it looked okay, but upon closer review the flaws stuck out immensely. I didn't want to tell anyone about my painful ordeals. What would they think of my flaws and imperfections? They already didn't like me. Does that sound familiar? Why would an all-knowing, wise God allow this type of pain?

He could have stopped it. It could make one wonder, "Does He love me? My mind has been filled with such anguish. How do I get free? They took my virginity before I was ready. The accident took my loved one. I was maimed in the fight. He left me. She denied and rejected my love. What do you do when time still hasn't healed the wound?" Jesus didn't let this tragic event sneak in, He had to give it permission to touch your life.

But God, wasn't there another way?

God says, "No, the devil thought he could kill you, and I knew he was no match for you."

You respond, "I didn't win; look at me I'm broken, dismayed, angry and confused.

"You're mine," says the Lord, "and when you allow me to touch your heart I will remove the pain."

"We could have avoided this Lord."

"No. You never would have known who I was in your life. You expressed your love deeply before the tragedy. You blew me kisses, you praised me with a full heart and your worship was unstoppable," He says.

"You think I let you go? You feel I have failed you?"

The Father responds, "Child, you're angry with me. I had to build you up; nothing is lost. Everything the devil thought he took I can replace in a greater abundance."

Don't be fooled; everything is controlled by the Lord. The devil denied it, but the book of Job tells us that the Lord allowed satan to harm Job. Job didn't understand and neither do we. However, in the broken place there is safety, restoration, healing, and love in abundance.

Peace resides here for the weary and faint of heart. Stop trying to figure it out and know that Christ is unchangeable, unstoppable, and unshakable. Right in the middle of your loss He will step in and lift you up. Maybe you don't think you can be lifted. Maybe your heart is hardened. It's okay. Nothing is bigger than God. What He began in you shall be completed. I know it is difficult.

Through flowing tears and pain, press until everything surrenders to His presence. I dare you to believe Him in the middle of your hardest fight. There is no other answer and no other way. Christ is the fullness of our provision. You have to believe against the odds. When hope has left, press, pray, and push. Every chain is broken; every hindered place is yielding.

Dryness is being flooded with the washing of the water of His word. It may feel like your worst test but you are going to make it. It's working for your good. Get ready! God has a blessing just for you. "I'm waiting," says the Lord. "I know your ending. I make all things new. Hold on. I never left; I have been silently awaiting your call. I'm here. Be healed in my presence."

I'm your answer, your friend, your mother, your father, whatever lack—I Am.

Read the Word, pray, run, but don't stay there. You may never understand, but I love you far greater than anyone ever could. Don't be afraid or angry any longer. It's over, declares the Lord.

God's grace and mercy is sufficient for me and you. Let us purpose to trust Christ even when we can't trace Him, and know that He reigns forever.

Declare & Decree: I will live and not die. I will declare the word of my Savior. I am restored and better than ever before. I am healed. I am whole. I am no longer crippled, broken, or paralyzed. ***IT'S OVER*** devil; I will rise up and live fully and completely. Thank You, Jesus! I am free!

Questions to Ponder
Week Twelve

1. What has God spoken to me that would help begin the healing process?

2. What does it mean to be made whole?

3. Why is it difficult to trust in the Lord for healing? What can I do to remove all doubt in his ability to heal and restore me?

4. How long have I been in the state? Why? What makes this time in my life different from others when I wallowed in the misery of my struggles, confusion, and pain?

5. What are things that I can do to fully believe God and oppose my circumstances?

   _____
   _____
   _____
   _____
   _____

6. In what ways can I recover from this tragic ordeal? What does the "healed" and "whole" me look like?

   _____
   _____
   _____
   _____
   _____

This week's prayers:

Lord, teach me to pray.
Lord, remove any doubt or unbelief.
Lord, destroy everything that I have allowed to take control of my life.

REFLECTION

Find scriptures on healing and allow the tragedy to be dismantled by His word.

For example: *He heals the brokenhearted and binds up their wounds.* (Psalm 147:3) I've tried talking to friends. I've even had few sessions of therapy where I was able to talk about my history of brokenness, but it is amazing to know that God can (and will) heal me of my broken heart. I must simply seek after it.

_____
_____
_____
_____
_____
_____
_____
_____
_____
_____
_____
_____
_____
_____
_____
_____
_____
_____
_____
_____
_____
_____
_____
_____
_____
_____

UN-MUTE
Week Thirteen

Scriptural Reference: Ecclesiastes 3:7 – A time to tear, and a time to sew, a time to keep silent, and a time to speak.

Focus: Take it off mute. Some are silenced by the hand of the enemy. Our voices have been quieted; we have not spoken in power and in might. We have not spoken above a whisper; we have stopped declaring that He is Lord. The devil comes to steal, kill, and destroy. Power is in our voices and we are called to declare the word, and to tell others about Jesus. Yet, we confess all that is wrong and broken. Our circumstances dictate our actions.

We won't believe God because it cost something to trust God. Let your silence be trampled by the power of the Lord. Shout loud, tell the world you're here. People need to hear your testimony; they need to know how you got over. Trust beyond what it looks like. I know that when your voice has been drowned out fear accompanies you and takes over. The Lord caused the blind to see the mute to speak and the deaf to hear. Women, the Lord commands you to open your mouth and tell the devil he is a liar. I will tell everyone about the goodness of Jesus. Now is the time to take it off mute and speak till the dead hear. Don't be persuaded in any other direction but a forward march.

> **INSIGHT**
>
> **The enemy has muzzled many of us to prevent us from speaking and witnessing to others. There is power in every testimony. Speak.**

I've found that many of us women have lost our ability to speak and not because of an accident or surgery. We stopped talking because our circumstances overwhelmed us. We became silent as we watched our lives fall apart. At first we were very vocal—yelling, screaming, and shouting. Finally things became too much and we became quiet.

Our voices were first lost in the garden when Eve engaged in conversation with the devil. After we lost that fight, the enemy of our souls snatched our voices. As women, we love to talk and express our feelings, talk about work, family, practically everything. Unless you were born into a culture where women aren't permitted to be very vocal, you understand that we talk a lot.

It's said that when a woman becomes quiet, watch out! So many painful things have caused our voices to slip away. Pain, frustration, hurt, and brokenness will shut us down. The Lord wants us to open our mouths and declare His greatness. Take it off mute! Don't allow anyone to back you into a corner. There are many who need to hear your words of wisdom, love, and encouragement.

People need to know who you are so speak up. The Lord gave us the command to tell the lost and dying that He is alive and well. Tell the world He is more than able to deliver them. Being in the grave is the only reason for silence. We have the ability to tell mountains to be removed and to cast out demons.

Cause the things that are wrong in our lives to fall dead by speaking it. Today, ladies, purpose to speak and start by telling the devil and your circumstances that it's over.

Declare & Decree: Lord, you are the lifter of my head and the restorer of my soul. Bless my voice so that others can hear me. I will not be quieted by my circumstances any longer.

Questions to Ponder
Week Thirteen

1. What are the dangers of being silent?

2. Who or what caused me to keep quiet?

3. What circumstances am I facing that produces fear?

4. How do I break free of the silence?

5. How do I find the boldness to declare the word of the Lord or to share my story with others?

REFLECTION

Find scriptures on sharing the word of God with others and purpose to cease the opportunity to do so.

For example: *And he said to them, "Go into all the world and proclaim the gospel to the whole creation."* (Mark 16:15) I am not ashamed. God has redeemed me from every negative emotion associated with my troublesome past. Now I'm setting out to help others.

VICTORY
Week Fourteen

Scriptural Reference: Deuteronomy 28:13 – And the Lord will make you the head and not the tail, you shall be above only and not beneath if you heed the commandments of the Lord your God. Which I command you today and are careful to observe them.

Focus: We are overcomers! If you have gone through this booklet, you have been on a 14-week journey to self-recognition—you've cried, changed, been released, empowered, and experienced a host of other emotions. My prayer now is that strength and power be poured into you so that you will live fully, whole, unhindered and unstoppable. Our Lord is calling for the bound, broken, troubled woman. He wants us whole, healed and filled with His spirit and our hands outstretched to help our sisters. There is nothing that the Lord wants more than for us to come out and then to pull our hurting sisters out of every plot, plan, trap and snare of the enemy. The very intent of his plan is broken off of your lives. As you begin to trust Him and fall in love with Him again, I pray restoration and peace flood your life. May you be increased to overflowing in Jesus name.

> INSIGHT
>
> Life's journey is filled with mountains and valleys, but if you hold fast, you will always arrive to your destination. Keep the faith. You are victorious.

Well, ladies, we have come to the end of one journey and are about to begin a new one. I wanted to give you my final words of encouragement. No one and nothing should stop you from accomplishing anything you want. You sit in a place of renewed power, strength and determination. Your vision should become very clear.

Take a deep breath; you are not the same woman. Though your situation may have been gloomy, hope should be overflowing inside you. God Himself has given us a new direction. We must listen for His voice. There are many devils that have tried and failed on many levels to stop Christ's plan for us. The devil cannot and will not ever succeed.

Greater is He who is in us than he who is in the world. Look again past your hurt, frustration, being overwhelmed, your lack, your disappointments and see change rising. Speak life into the atmosphere of your lives and command change. God has not given us the spirit of fear, but of power, of love, and of a sound mind. You may have been going crazy, but it's over.

The storm, the rage, the bark of the devil is done. The Kingdom of Heaven suffers violence and the violent take it by force. We have power and dominion over the earth and all that's in it. It's time that we take what's ours and stop waiting for someone to give it to us. The devil is clear in his plan of destruction for us.

Let us be clear in our Father's plan of redemption. He loves us! What more do you need than that? God is able; He won't fail.

Declare & Decree: I am more than a conqueror through Jesus Christ. I am empowered to win. The past can't hold me and my future is bright. Today is a new day and I my vision has been renewed.

Questions to Ponder
Week Fourteen

1. Were these lessons a blessing to you? Which ones were most effective in this season?

2. Did you find any lesson more difficult than others?

3. What did you discover about yourself?

4. Are there indications that you've been set free from anything at the completion of this workbook?

5. Are you ready for the new season in your life? What is your vision for the future? What are some of your immediate goals?

_____
_____
_____
_____
_____
_____

REFLECTION

Locate scriptures about being victorious and apply them to your life as you continue to live victoriously through Jesus Christ.

For example: *But thanks be to God, who gives us the victory through our Lord Jesus Christ.* (I Corinthians 15:57) Today, I want to take time out to simply praise God for who He is and appreciate the many trials that He has helped me to overcome.

ABOUT THE AUTHOR

Evangelist Oneida Martin is a former drug prevention counselor with the Department of Education where she served those in her community for 30 years. For 25 years, Oneida has counseled students and their families on issues of gang awareness, self-esteem, teen pregnancy, grief, and child abuse amongst other things. Oneida's goal was to teach students that no matter the circumstances they can overcome if they believe in themselves.

Evangelist Oneida has been saved since 1984. She has endured many adversities including molestation, painful marriage, brokenness, despair. Leaning on and trusting in her Lord and Savior, Jesus Christ, is what has given her the courage and ability to push forward. Oneida is a preacher, teacher, mentor, and praise and worship leader. She heads the women's ministry in her church, is an intercessor, and has a gift to help those who are demonically oppressed be set free.

Oneida is a writer, expressing the power of Christ love and healing through her words penned in love. Oneida's passion is to become what Apostle Paul strove for: all things to all men, women, children that she might win some. Oneida loves helping broken women regain their voice and footing by sharing the message that Christ still saves, heals, delivers, and sets free.

www.ingramcontent.com/pod-product-compliance
Lightning Source LLC
Chambersburg PA
CBHW022121040426
42450CB00006B/790